You're Not Too Old

A Collection of Poems
For Senior Citizens

Barbara Ferguson

You're Not Too Old
A Collection of Poems for Senior Citizens
By Barbara Ferguson

Copyright © 2014.
All rights reserved.

No part of this publication may be reproduced, stored in a retrieval system, or transmitted—electronic, mechanical, photocopy, recording, or any other way—without the written prior permission of the copyright holder, except as permitted by US copyright law.

First Printing: January 2014

Foreword

As long as we are alive, we can do our part to make the world a better place.

We anticipate retirement with hopes and dreams. With extra time, all the knowledge we've gained through the years, and friends we've made, this can be the happiest time of our lives. Moving out of a familiar routine can be both intimidating and exciting.

I have spent over half of my life as a widow. After I retired, there were many decisions to make. I left the security of my comfort zone. It took courage to make changes. I chose to move near a son to be involved in the lives of my grandchildren during their formative years. I needed to make new friends and find new activities that were fun and challenging. I enjoy helping people, cooking, and expressing my thoughts poetically. There is no one-size-fits-all solution. Your story will be different.

Living alone, I often express my observations and feelings on paper. One poem is a spontaneous response to a beautiful sunrise. Some are more serious, like surviving the physical challenges of the aging process, or breaking a bad habit. A few are informative, like explaining what we do in the flexercize class I lead. Others embrace life lessons I've learned from a squirrel or apricot tree. The "Canine Kennel" antics and "Going Green" are just for fun.

This book has been written with the hope that it will bring a smile to your face, inspire you to enjoy the best quality of life possible, and give you ideas that will help you prioritize time and resources for maximum satisfaction in senior living.

Enjoy *You're Not Too Old*.

Dedication

This book is dedicated to fellow senior citizens who are seeking to maximize their potential for the rest of their lives.

I'm grateful for the friends at the Senior Center and North Texas Christian Writers who encouraged me to share these poems—especially Frank Ball, Sandra Bonham, Flo Chism, Victoria Fairfield, and Kay Smith, who helped edit them.

I'm grateful to Suzi Harvey for sharing the cover picture of her husband on his final family vacation to Hawaii. J D is sitting on the island, looking over the unlimited expanse of the Pacific Ocean. This illustrates a retiree looking into the future with its unknown potential, ready to begin exploring.

"They shall still bear fruit in old age:
They shall be fresh and flourishing."
Psalm 92:14 (NKJV)

Preface

As a very giving person, Barbara Ferguson is lovingly sharing with us a glimpse of herself through poetry. I say "us" because she shared her poems with friends as she lived them... and we loved them and looked forward to the next one. I am so glad she is publishing this book so you can look forward to each one, and hopefully continue to share them as well. Be inspired, challenged, and enjoy all that is offered in this collection. If God allows, "we" might just have Volume II someday.

Kay Smith

Disclaimer

This book contains something for everyone.
Those who look for errors ought to have fun.
This is one of every writer's worst fears;
There will still be mistakes after editing for years.
I'm publishing while seniors still know how to look,
And turn paper pages in an old-fashioned book

You're Not Too Old . .

    . . . to Be of Value

    . . . to Enjoy Retirement

    . . . to Appreciate Grandchildren

    . . . to Flourish Mentally and Spiritually

    . . . to Cherish old Memories

    . . . to Care for your Health

    . . . to Live Alone

    . . . to Downsize

    . . . to Prepare for leaving Planet Earth

Table of Contents

Sunrise _____ 1

How I Thrive Past 75 _____ 2

You're Not Too Old! _____ 4

Inclined to Decline _____ 5

How Important Are You? _____ 6

Increasing in Value _____ 7

I Want My Life to Count _____ 8

Dementia is Not Beyond God's Love _____ 9

ReTire for an Amazing Journey _____ 10

The Adventure of a Lifetime _____ 12

Mentoring Young Women _____ 14

Airport Security _____ 15

Confrontation _____ 16

Microwave Generation _____ 17

New Challenges _____ 18

Prepare for Your Once-in-a-Lifetime Adventure ___ 20

Enjoy Your Golden Years _____ 22

Barrel Racing _____ 23

Trampoline	24
Christmas Tree Pretzels	25
Canine Kennel	26
Modern Study Hall	28
Connect Four	29
Evan Mows	30
Computer Tech	31
Lemonade Stand	32
It's Only a Test	33
Birthdays: The Extreme Makeover	34
Pruning the Tree	36
Close to the Master	38
Life Won't Always Be Easy	39
Don't Give Up	40
Emotional Preparation for Aging	43
Stress	44
Learning to Relax	45
Why Let Stress Cause Distress?	46
Is Your Cup Full?	48
Jesus, the Pacesetter	49

Crisis: Calm or Chaos?	50
Waterfall	52
Indecisive Squirrel	55
Peace and Joy	56
Fall Colors	57
Let's Skip Fall This Year	58
Bruised Lip and Ego	59
Cataract Surgery	60
Flexercize Class	62
Is Pain Free What I Will Always Be?	64
Suffering	66
Healthy Balance	68
Accidents	70
Going Green	71
Husband to the Widow	72
Cooking for One Can Be Fun	74
Missy	76
Guests	77
Financial Fitness	78
Drastic with Plastic	79

Attitude Toward Aging	80
Caregivers	81
Spring Training	82
When There's a Will, There's a Way To Get Through a Tough Day	85
Time for the Big Move	86
Assisted Living	88
Happy Birthday, Sis	90
Those Senior Moments	91
God's Kingdom is Here	92
The New Heaven and Earth	95
Humor Goes a Long Way	96
About the Author and Book	97

Sunrise

Each morning greets me with a pleasant surprise.
The sky, a vast canvas with a gorgeous sunrise.

The Lord enjoys color, the full spectrum He uses,
To display His vast glory each day as He chooses.

God says, "Good morning, this is a new day.
Come walk with me, and I'll show you the way."

He shines a big light so I can see where I'm going:
Provides spiritual food to keep me growing.

At the close of the day, so I won't forget,
He paints the sky with a spectacular sunset.

How I Thrive Past 75

How does this senior try to stay young?
There certainly is nothing wrong with my tongue.
I can make phone calls to encourage a friend,
But I'm no good with the new texting trend.

When I first wake up, if I'm not in pain,
I creatively write what's on my brain.
Early in the morning I ride my bike,
For the coolest part of the day I like.

After breakfast I spend time with the Lord.
I share my feelings: excited or bored.
I read the Bible for strength for the day
And feel His presence and peace as I pray.

God gives ideas for plenty to do,
I anxiously start when my quiet time's through.
On Monday and Friday I work at the church,
But I'm no good with an Internet search.

Wednesday join friends at the senior lunch.
Thursday I lead an exercise bunch.
Once a month I attend writer's critique.
Baking Sunday snacks ends a typical week.

During the school year a job that is cool,
Is crossing guard at a nearby school.
Much satisfaction retirement brings,
I get to do all of my favorite things.

I attend grandchildren's concerts and games,
But it's hard to remember all their friends' names.
I no longer play games with kids on the floor.
Besides trouble getting up, my legs get too sore.

Cataracts affect my eyesight,
So I'd rather not drive my car at night.
I'm slowing down a little perhaps,
For I sure enjoy brief afternoon naps.

Occasionally arthritis will hit
And slow me down for a little bit.
But God has always been so good to me
That I want to be the best I can be.

You're Not Too Old!

How long has it been since you were told?
"You can't do that, you're too old."
It's often said with derisive scorn,
But, we all started aging the day we were born.
At sixty-five when your vocation is done
Don't retire from life, but relax and have fun.
You could help kids cross the street after school.
Delivering meals-on-wheels might be cool.

You might teach a girl to cook or sew,
Or a boy some maintenance skills you know.
The very wisest decision by far
Is to serve others right where you are.
When joints are hurting, you want to sit still.
When pain gets oppressive, don't just take a pill.
This way unused muscles deteriorate,
And then the pain gets unbearably great.

Don't waste your money on younger looks.
Just keep your mind active with puzzles and books.
You've gained much wisdom
By the time you're this age.
It didn't disappear when you stop earning a wage.
Apply all this wisdom to maintain your health.
Fewer trips to the doctor will extend your wealth.
Exercise and eat healthy to keep muscles strong.
Enjoy friends in the neighborhood where you belong.

Inclined to Decline

If identity depends upon what you do,
Then advancing age will be hard on you.
After many years, parts begin to wear out.
Don't be surprised, wondering what it's about.

At a slower pace, you will be seeing
You're not a human doing, but a human being.
As a child of God, you've reached a new stage.
You're valuable to Him, regardless of age.

Submit to your Father as your child did you.
You'll enjoy new adventures you're going through.
Just cuddle up in your Father's embrace,
Secure as you bring a smile to His face.

Let God be your lover, protector, provider.
Let pain and loneliness be the outsider.
Slowing down from the race you have run,
You'll like to hear God say, "My child, well done."

How Important Are You?

Thank You, Father, for sending a Savior
To rescue us from destructive behavior.
I'm glad the Creator of the universe
Came to earth to reverse the curse.

Jesus came in such an ordinary way,
That many missed Him, and still do today.
Some consider their resources enough
To take care of all the important stuff.

Since we are more than body, mind, and soul,
We need God's Spirit to make us whole.
Even if we're adequate here on earth,
Death would be tragic without a new birth.

God gifted uniquely as part of His plan
To provide for, protect, and bless every man.
But when a person leaves God out of his life,
He will battle both insecurity and strife.

Not doing our part will impact everyone,
While working together we'll get the job done.
A puzzle satisfies with each piece in place.
So does God's plan for the human race.

But we get to choose if we'll live God's way
To obediently walk in His strength each day.
Obviously God would prefer that we do,
But obedience is up to me and to you.

Increasing in Value

In a throw-away culture when value is lost,
Into the trash can the item is tossed.
But people are valuable to the end,
Especially when Jesus is their best Friend.

When I am old, He won't cast me away.
In weakness and trouble, I can still pray.
When I'm mistreated by an evil one,
A just God will see that justice is done.

There's no other god who can compare
With Jehovah God who is everywhere.
He's holy and righteous and available,
Trustworthy, strong, and dependable.

He teaches me all that I need to know,
And guides and protects me wherever I go.
I will praise Him as long as I live
And share with others what He wants to give.

When life here is over, God still will save
And lovingly bring me up from the grave.
He has a place prepared just for me
Where I'll live with Him for eternity.

I Want My Life to Count

Sometimes I'm depressed as I think about
What I used to do when I could get out.
I used to stress, now it's just You and me.
Help me feel secure in Your company.

Content with what You give me to do,
It's not about me, Lord, it's all about You.
You put me exactly where You want me to be
To use for Your purpose effectively.

You provide talents that I need to use,
And give me the privilege to choose,
To work with You, or by myself.
To bring glory to You, or stay on a shelf.

Lord, I don't want to barely survive,
But to be active and fully alive.
I can't do all things I used to do,
But that doesn't mean my life here is through.

Since I will reap just what I sow,
I will spread kindness wherever I go.
As an older woman I should be
An example to young ones watching me.

Modeling how to be givers, not takers,
To love their families as good homemakers.
Joyfully fulfilling Your plan for me,
As I journey toward eternity.

Dementia is Not Beyond God's Love

I'm glad my sister has a room of her own
With familiar pictures and even her phone.
She's always done well--a perfectionist--
Meticulous housekeeping she will insist.

She'll pick up trash whether it's there or not
Because she's repulsed by a dirty spot.
With poor depth perception, she often will fall.
She refuses to use her walker at all.

She seemed to enjoy my visit today.
I sang some hymns, then she wandered away.
Often her words are unintelligible,
But she still is very valuable.

I'll honor and love her with memories shared
And try to console her when she is scared.
Though lapses of memory often occur,
She may forget God, but He won't forget her.

ReTire for an Amazing Journey

People disillusioned with the way their lives went,
Eagerly anticipate retirement.
They believe the popular fantasy
They'll do what they please, since they will be free.

No salary comes in, but still bills to pay.
They're wise if they've put some money away.
Without the corporate ladder to climb
They think they will have a lot more time.

A new set of challenges also arrives.
Health issues begin to affect their lives.
Some friends may move, others pass away,
Or babysit grandchildren most of the day.

If you're frustrated and don't know what to do
Then find somebody as lonely as you.
Get active in church or your senior center.
A neighbor child might need a good mentor.

Your lifetime of wisdom be willing to share
With grace and compassion
which shows that you care.
Activities and venues may need to change,
New goals and commitments
at first may seem strange.

Right now you may not have the slightest clue,
But God still has a good plan for you.
You want your life here to be effective,
And have value from God's perspective.

The Adventure of a Lifetime

Preparing for this once-in-a-lifetime adventure,
I think about all of the things that I treasure.
Grandchildren's sports I enjoy from the stands,
Without trips to practice that little league demands.

I enjoy a band concert played in harmony,
Without listening to practice sounds repeatedly.
There is time for a game or a cooking spree.
I have wisdom to share, if they ever ask me.

Another issue is responsibility.
There's less laundry to do, since it's only me.
I don't track in dirt like the kids used to do,
So daily housework is minimized, too.

The food that I cook lasts several meals,
A valuable time saver that also appeals.
No need for make-up or to dress up each day,
No longer in the public and working for pay.

I can sleep late, since no alarm do I choose.
Eat breakfast in front of TV watching the news.
There's flexibility for investing my time.
No boss to please, no corporate ladder to climb.

In beautiful weather my bike I can ride.
In extreme temperatures I stay inside.
Cell phones don't rule me, I don't tweet or text,
And won't wait in line for what's coming next.

Warning: Possible Side Effects

Unfortunately life isn't all fun and games.
Sometimes I can't even remember friend's names.
Loose dentures clack when I try to talk.
I need cane or walker to help me walk.
Squeaky hearing aids are a nuisance for me.
Print in the phone book is too small to see.
Arthritis sneaks in to attack joints with pain.
Slowing down reduces output, so what did I gain?

No longer stressed by our culture's rat race,
I'll enjoy life at a l e i s u r e l y pace.

Mentoring Young Women

Don't think life is over because you've turned gray.
Let me share what happened to me yesterday.
A Home Helper I met at the senior center
Is an orphan who needs a mom for a mentor.

She is about the age of my son.
A daughter who likes to talk could be fun.
She brought me flowers, honored me like a queen,
Took me to dinner with visiting between.

She shared from her heart and then we prayed.
She faced some problems and was afraid.
God has gifted her, so He has a plan.
It would be nice if it includes a man.

As a mature widow living alone,
It's tempting to focus on things of my own.
But there are young women struggling out there
Who need love and guidance from seniors who care.

With grown sons my routines are rearranged,
And many activities have been changed,
As I share what I've learned through the years
I can encourage through problems and fears.

I can share how God faithfully guides
And the comfort He always provides.
This season of life doesn't just go one way,
I must graciously receive from others today.

Airport Security

Ever since the terrorist fright,
Airport security has been tight.
I don't mind taking off my shoes.
Bending to re-tie, I'd like to refuse.

I was thrilled at the airport today,
When I saw a sign in the entry way.
"Age 75 needn't take off their shoes."
What a pleasant surprise! Very good news!

Confrontation

Where is My Security?

Confrontation is hard for me.
I prefer encouraging others, you see.
Like Jonah, I'd rather share God's blessing
Than point out sins that need confessing.
They'll probably say, "Who are you to judge?
Our way is working, so why should we budge?"

Before I have their permission to start,
The Holy Spirit must convict their heart.
That this is from God, they must believe
In order to repent and then to receive.
God wants them to go a different way
To experience His love and freedom today.

If I tell, they can't claim they haven't heard,
But I fear rejection if they spurn my word.
But what if like Nineveh they do repent?
Won't that be valuable time well spent?
Unlike Jonah, I don't want to disobey
And cause more trouble by running away.

God, I confess that I am afraid.
I need strength and courage, lest I evade
This opportunity to speak for You,
And share the message You've asked me to.
But first please deal with the need in me,
To trust You alone for security.

Microwave Generation

I fear a microwave generation
Is taking over our wonderful nation.
As farmers we knew that we all would need
To wait for harvest after planting a seed.
Weeding and watering never were through,
So passively waiting would not do.

Now when we want something we drive to the store.
There's never enough, we always want more.
When money runs low we pull out the plastic,
If we were wise, we'd do something drastic.
In an emergency when we're in a mess,
We should consider living on less.

We'd be better off with a little less noise,
And fewer new electronic toys.
What has happened to polite conversation?
Or families enjoying a nice vacation?
Before we tumble over the brink
Priorities we should seriously rethink.

Most people consider this rather odd:
The Bible says to be still so we can know God.
His Word contains wisdom for His unique plan.
He puts His Spirit within each saved man.
He may say to wait in a still small voice.
He prefers we obey, but He gives us the choice.

New Challenges

Remember what you said
When your child said, "I can't"?
If you knew he could,
You weren't deterred by his rant.
You carefully instructed and guided each step.
When basics were mastered,
What excitement and pep!

Why do we resist our Heavenly Father?
If He didn't think we could, why would He bother?
The challenges of aging are scary for us,
But we can go through them without a big fuss.

Were you not happy when your child would try
New challenges, rather than give up and cry?
When he would try, you both had more fun.
He gained satisfaction, so both of you won.

I want to listen for my Father's voice,
And quickly say "Yes" when He gives me a choice.
In this season with new things to be learned.
I need to shed baggage with which I'm concerned.

There've always been things
Which were not much fun,
But we did them because they had to be done.
Many things change with every new season.
Developing character is the main reason.

The clock will keep ticking, whatever we do.
Outcome depends upon response from you.
Circumstance fluctuates but you have the choice:
Will you fight aging, or accept and rejoice?

Prepare for Your Once-in-a-Lifetime Adventure

As we grow older, there are adjustments to make,
For us, our companions—for everyone's sake.
We need to downsize, getting rid of some stuff,
So cleaning and finding things won't be so rough.
A place for all things, everything in its place,
Will save lots of time if that truth we embrace.

As senses grow weaker, food won't taste as well.
Air freshener and mints might help with the smell.
As cataracts begin to mess with the eyes,
Driving at night is probably unwise.
Conversation is hard with hearing impaired.
Increase the phone volume so you'll be prepared.

We know that this trip will eventually come,
So not preparing would be rather dumb.
Think of some things you probably will need
And begin to plant desirable seed.
Thoughtful compassion pays rich dividends
If you must relocate and make some new friends.

If you began healthy habits years ago
You will keep active although you move slow.
Cooking was more fun with a family to share;
You still can eat healthy with less food to prepare.
Brushing and flossing prolong natural teeth use,
Listen to your body, but don't just make excuse.

Do something creative—paint, garden, or write.
Rest during the day, as well as at night.
Enjoy precious memories made in the past,
But live in the present, for time will go fast.
Plan for the future and help family prepare
For the time when you will no longer be there.

Because activities and places must change,
Don't get upset or think it too strange.
Have you become a congenial host?
For you are the person you'll be with the most.
That will determine your pleasure in old age,
As your life drama plays on a different stage.

Enjoy Your Golden Years

If you spend too long just sitting still
You'll soon discover it makes you ill.
Muscles tend to deteriorate,
Aided by the junk food that you ate.

Don't selfishly consume or hoard your wealth.
Invest in activities for your health.
Exercise muscles to keep them strong.
Cultivate friends so you will belong.

Let games and books stimulate your brain,
Then more of your memory will remain.
Resolve issues quickly to minimize fears,
So you can enjoy your golden years.

Barrel Racing

My friends participate in the barrel race
On horses, in arenas, with lots of space.
They ride in the shape of a three leaf clover.
Before they know it, the race is over.

Each morning I'm involved in a barrel race,
Between orange barrels with limited space.
Although my horses have much more power,
I only go twenty miles per hour.

My friends say barrel racing is fun.
I hope this construction soon is done.
Even when this project is complete,
The barrels will just roll down the street.

Since there always will be construction some place,
We might as well get used to the barrel race.
It makes impatient drivers quite mad.
Their lack of concern for workers is sad.

They opened the round-about today.
No barrels or arrows to show me the way.
Now that this road construction is done,
The Trophy Lake Speedway has begun.

Trampoline

I don't aspire to the younger scene,
But I joined my grandson on the trampoline.

One day we bounced a little too high.
I fell and hurt my neck and thigh.

The doctor gave me a cortisone shot.
Then the *old lady lecture* was what I got.

"It's time to enter retirement mode.
Medicare has no trampoline accident code."

So my trampoline jumping days were done.
It was time to find other grandson fun.

Christmas Tree Pretzels

One Christmas when I visited my son,
I thought of a project that might be fun.
While parents shopped for gifts for their bunch,
I stayed with the children to fix their lunch.

The girls and I had a secret plan,
A gift for their favorite woman and man.
I furnished the pretzels and almond bark.
Girls added green coloring to make it dark.

The microwave melted the candy so we
Could cover each pretzel Christmas tree.
Waxed paper covered the kitchen shelves.
Aprons protected fronts of Santa's elves.

Did I tell you the girls were three and two?
Neatness they had not yet learned to do.
Production went well till quality control
Sampled the product that came from the bowl.

Green faces on elves began to appear
With almond bark smiles from ear to ear.
We managed to save a few little trees.
A gift for parents they wanted to please.

Global warming was in the kitchen that day.
Not sure if you'd call it labor or play.
We actually saved a tree or two.
The kitchen was *green* when we were through.

Canine Kennel

(The Tail of Two Dogs)

My spring break
Had a different take
Than that of my kids who went skiing.
The day of the rain
It was a pain
Wiping paws after dogs were out peeing.

But mostly they lay
In the backyard all day
Soaking up vitamin D.
After rolling around
In the grass on the ground,
My carpet was a sight to see.

They got along great
Except Penny ate
Cookie's food after she finished hers.
So I'd save Cookie's food
Till Penny's sun bathing mood
And Cookie's inside time occurs.

Jealously arose
When Penny's nose
Would rest on my lap to be pet.
Cookie came in between
And made quite a scene
"Me too—and don't you forget!"

Each black and white dog
Slept like a log
All night curled up in her place.
But when morning came
And I called her name,
To the back door both dogs would race.

Meanwhile each master
Seeing who could go faster
Down the ski slopes in cold Santa Fe,
Got stuck in the snow
And had to go slow,
So they didn't make it home in one day.

Their final uniting
Was so exciting
I've never seen tails wagging faster.
When they first got their scent
They knew what it meant,
Each soon would go home with her master.

As a steady diet
I prefer the quiet,
Though that week I enjoyed company instead.
But today I have time
For this silly rhyme
That keeps running through my dog gone head.

Modern Study Hall

I enjoyed studying with my grandson last night
On the half-bath floor with no air, but good light.
School these days doesn't seem quite the same.
It resembles a computer game.
Instead of writing a history report,
He did power point in our little fort.

The electronic notebook certainly looks
Much lighter than a backpack full of books.
Quite different from the way school was in my day.
Study was definitely separate from play.
A notebook contained everything I would need.
Penmanship essential so teachers could read.

Looking hours at a screen wouldn't be wise.
That glare and small print are too hard on my eyes.
I'm glad these students can creatively use
Little spaces to study, if they so choose.
I'm glad they're learning to use technology,
But the old fashioned way worked better for me.

Connect Four

I remember when we played Connect Four
In the dark closet sitting on the floor.
Evan would give me the pretty orange stack
While he always chose the dark ugly black.
The way he would hold the flashlight to see,
Helped him see my orange, but didn't help me.

Before I knew it, the game would be done.
I couldn't see black, so he always won.
I always acted like it was a surprise,
And gave him credit for being quite wise.
My grandson is real creative and bright.
He never challenged me in the daylight.

Evan Mows

Lawn work is needed every week or so.
My grandson comes to my house to mow.
I'm sorry I don't have a riding mower.
Just have a broom, no fancy blower.

Thank you Evan for the job that you do.
You stay at the task until you are through.
When you finish you sweep up the mess.
I'm impressed with your hard work
and thoughtfulness.

You're learning skills you will use for years
In most honorable careers.
Observing a problem. Meeting a need.
Doing your best. Then you will succeed.

Computer Tech

Sometimes David would go to the school
To take Jordan home, which he thought was cool.
"We have a family emergency.
I need to take Jordan home with me."

"Shall we get Bethany out of her class?"
"No, only Jordan will need the hall pass."
Dave only could work if his computer did,
Which needed the ability of this kid.

A knack for computers Jordan always had.
He fixed Dad's equipment when it went bad.
Then returned to school for the rest of the day.
Teachers glad now everything seemed okay.

Lemonade Stand

An entrepreneur when only eight.
For morning light she could hardly wait.
Bethany had a lemonade stand.
Responsibility it did demand.

At night we went to the grocery store
For lemonade, cups, and a few items more.
Jordan's birthday gift was motivation
For that job during summer vacation.

An active young lady she'll always be,
College or habitat for humanity.
Well organized and extremely bright.
Time spent with Bethany is a delight.

It's Only a Test

The tornado siren blares. Not a cloud in the sky. "This is only a test," is announced over the loud speaker. I ignore it and go about my business. Why can't I do the same with other unpleasant noises in my life, and remember that they are "only a test"?

Solomon said, "Nothing new under the sun."
So when problems come, I shouldn't get undone.
There also will be a way through the mess
So why does a problem cause such distress?
My car failed its first inspection this year.
The bumper got scratched when a car got too near.
The shower grout caused a leak on the floor.
I need to repair the crumbling shed door.
Today something went quite wrong with my knee,
So I'm not as active as I'd like to be.
In the recliner with knee under ice
There's time to consider his wise advice.
No hopeless problem: **it's only a test**.
Will I respond with worry or rest?
I've had bigger problems than any of these.
Walking with God through them should be a breeze.
When a friend came to visit, in slithered a snake.
A challenge demanding quick action to take.
Others need counsel and more time to pray,
That God will show me the very best way.
Since there is "Nothing new under the sun",
It helps to recall God's past victories won.

Birthdays: The Extreme Makeover

For children, birthdays are a lot of fun.
I used to anticipate every one.
Each year would measure how much I had grown
And gained new freedoms to be on my own.

Somewhere around sixty it seemed to start
That several things began falling apart.
My legs no longer wanted to hurry.
My eyes began to fade and get blurry.

Voices on the phone no longer were clear.
I wouldn't admit that I couldn't hear.
An orthopedist replaced my right knee.
Cataracts were removed to help me see.

My teeth were traded for dentures instead
That I remove before going to bed.
The audiologist put a thing in my ear.
Sometimes it squeals, but at least I can hear.

No organs need a transplant quite yet,
But if that time comes, I probably will get.
Extreme makeovers are now in fashion.
I am made over with a new passion.

While the physical parts are wearing out,
The spiritual part becomes more devout.
Instead of selfishly thinking of me,
More needs in others I'm starting to see.

When problems arise, rather than get mad,
The joy of the Lord helps me to be glad.
The Great Physician has a wonderful plan:
Extreme makeovers for each woman and man.

Medical doctors help bodies on earth,
But only the Lord provides a new birth.
Instead of frustration with what I can't do,
God asks me to try some things that are new.

And while the younger set whisper and gloat
We smile, for someday they'll be in our boat.
I'll enjoy birthdays as they comes along.
One day they will stop—but today I am strong.

Pruning the Tree

My mother had a fruit tree many years ago.
Bare branches in the winter
Were covered up with snow.
As south winds welcomed springtime,
White blossoms would appear.
Without another freeze,
There were apricots that year.

One year the tree was loaded:
The trunk just split in two.
Men propped up limbs with two by fours
Till harvest time was through.
They wrapped a chain around the trunk
So it could heal itself,
While apricots I picked and canned
To store on pantry shelf.

That winter when the limbs were bare,
The pruning job began.
Large fruit on fewer branches
Yielded just as much to can.
If that tree could tell
About the pruning it endured,
The temporal pain was worth
The larger apricots procured.

I'm like that little branch
That held so many apricots.
When the load's too heavy,
It just ties me up in knots.
I need help to prop me up
Until my wounds can heal.
Resting for a season,
Brings more energy and zeal.

As God does His pruning,
Non-essentials have to go,
So there will be sufficient space
For larger fruit to grow.
I often try to dodge the shears
When branches must be cut.
But later I can clearly see
I'd gotten in a rut.

Jesus is the Living Vine
My branch depends upon.
Without His life within me,
I could truly not go on.
God knows His future plan for me,
How pruning will allow
His life to yield more fruit in me,
Though I can't see it now.

Close to the Master

A lady out walking her dog today,
Walked steadily on the sidewalk way.
Her tail-wagging dog was by her side
Until a moving sight he spied.

The morning walk began quite well
Until a whiff of an unknown smell,
Lured him away from his master's side,
Till choked by the chain with which he was tied.

This called attention to the choice he made.
A painful reminder that he had strayed.
A vivid picture of what happens to me
While walking with Jesus adoringly.

When something draws my attention away,
I get involved and neglect to pray.
Then something painful brings conviction to me,
That close to my Master is where I should be.

Life Won't Always Be Easy

I'm sure many times Joseph wanted to scream,
"This is no way, Lord, to fulfill that dream!
Nice things were supposed to pave the way
For me to be honored by brothers someday."

After thirteen hard years, Joseph was surprised
By the detours he took till the dream was realized.
I'm glad he trusted the God he couldn't see,
For his faithful life has inspired me.

When adversity came, and tempted to doubt,
I would beg God for an easy way out.
Problems got worse with nothing I could do,
But depend upon God to help me get through.

In retrospect, God was molding me
For an exciting future opportunity.
It wouldn't have been possible years ago,
Without the challenges that helped me grow.

Now I can see how God often will use
Adversity to build character when I choose
To stay close and trust Him
While going through a test.
Focused on Jesus, I'm ultimately blessed.

Don't Give Up

When we get to the end of our rope,
We shouldn't give up, there always is hope.
We'll never wind up anywhere
That God is not already there.

In a self-centered world of greed and strife,
God wants for us an abundant life.
He is a Father who really cares
And wants involvement in our affairs.

He uniquely created each woman and man
For a good place in His overall plan.
We shouldn't try everything on our own,
Or face life's challenges alone.

We need to listen to God's kind voice.
Seek council before we make a choice.
Admit our need, and in Him confide.
His Word, true wisdom will provide.

Is love and acceptance what we're looking for,
Or significance, value, or something more?
The Lord will gladly meet every need.
With inner strength so we can proceed.

Don't count on riches or worldly fame,
They fluctuate, never stay the same.
But God will meet our needs forever
In a way no circumstance can sever.

God does not change, His love will last.
He won't keep bringing up our past.
If our repentance was sincere,
We need no longer live in fear.

I couldn't pay the debt myself.
God doesn't want me on a shelf.
He created me to be a light
To shine His love in this world's dark night.

God wants a relationship that is nice,
That's why Jesus paid such a big price
We all deserve to die for our sin.
Christ takes our place when invited in.

In the beginning, all life was good,
Operating just the way it should.
With a special love between God and man
Everything went according to plan.

Man forgot God had made him from clay,
Thought he knew best, so did not obey.
Faced with life choices, what will we do?
Focus on problems, worry, or stew?

Or will we let God help us take a stand
To let His light shine in this needy land?
God wisely had an overall plan.
Which Christ demonstrated on earth as a man.

For abundant life that frees from sin,
God's Spirit will strengthen us within.
God spoke the universe into being.
Christ offers more than what we are seeing.

God in Heaven directs mission control.
Christ died for sin so we could be whole.
The Holy Spirit resides in each soul.
Living the Spirit-filled life is our goal.

Emotional Preparation for Aging

You may not want an antique celebration,
But at least you can make some preparation.
Old age will come someday, make no mistake,
So plan ahead for everyone's sake.

If you live long enough, the chances are
You won't reach old age without a scar.
Take care of wounds when they first appear,
So they won't get uglier year after year.

Probably someone has been unfair
Or treated you wrong and didn't care.
Forgive them and their offense release,
Or bitterness will consume, rather than peace.

No one enjoys a grumpy old man.
Cultivate positive traits while you can.
Then people will relish being with you,
And you'll enjoy life while you're passing through.

Stress

How can a person live without stress
When everything seems to be in a mess?
Don't just take pills so you can go faster.
Turn to the Lord, let Him be your Master.
Nobody thinks that what he does is wrong,
But faithful integrity will keep him strong.

Don't try to get by with the least you can do,
Wholeheartedly work to make dreams come true.
Selfish entitlement grabs all it can.
By thinking of others, you value each man.
Encourage friends to do what they do best
And trust in the Lord to do all the rest.

For people depressed, lonely or bored,
There's no substitute for walking with the Lord.
God knows all about you and dearly loves you,
And has an assignment for you to do.
If you'll let Jesus, He'll be your guide.
Listen to His Holy Spirit inside.

The fruit of the Spirit is love, joy, and peace.
His adequate grace, will your stress release.
You see, God created everything good.
It's best when we operate as we should.
Unfortunately some fail to discover
That life is best with God as their Lover.

Learning to Relax

Jesus didn't stress, so why should I?
He took time for people as He passed by.
Why in the world do I insist
On doing everything on my to-do list?

Why not schedule a leisurely minute
So when there's a need I'm available in it?
I'm learning a truth as a crossing guard.
I needn't feel bad when a job isn't hard.

I'm doing what I was hired to do,
Even if I only help cross a few.
This lesson isn't so hard for me,
When Jesus is my priority.

Why Let Stress Cause Distress?

When stress has me all uptight
So I cannot sleep at night,
Whatever pressure's in the way,
Tomorrow is another day.

Work God assigns, He will provide
Because His Spirit lives inside.
To give me wisdom for each task,
All I need to do is ask.

With much to do, I tend to worry.
Driven by deadlines, I start to hurry.
I make more mistakes and waste more time
When alertness needs to be at its prime.

I am responsible to separate
My will from God's that's on my plate.
If daily by His plan I live,
In crises, extra strength He'll give.

Our Father loves His kids so much,
He always wants to stay in touch.
He sees the challenges ahead,
And plans alternate routes instead.

With food and rest and exercise,
Time in God's Word to make me wise,
Holding no anger or fear inside,
God's love and peace will abide.

When tensions arise or I'm afraid,
I remind myself this day God made.
My Father is with me every minute;
I will rejoice and be glad in it.

Is Your Cup Full?

Is positive or negative the strongest pull?
Is your cup half empty? Or is it half full?
When clouds dump on you an inch of rain,
Do you thank God? Or do you complain?

When your heart and lungs are working right,
Do you gripe with a tiny mosquito bite?
There will always be tension between good and bad.
We can enjoy peace, or we can be sad.

With every good gift comes responsibility.
Focus determines what our perspective will be.
I prefer to choose Jesus, the one in control
Who has a good plan, heading for the right goal.

Many factors contribute to who we are now,
DNA and attitude intertwine somehow.
We can choose the direction our life will take.
Will we be transparent or just be a fake?

We've had bumps and bruises along the way
That helped determine who we are today.
It's never too late to change direction,
And to receive God's abundant affection.

Jesus, the Pacesetter

Why do we want things bigger and faster?
Doesn't that cause financial disaster?
Wouldn't everything be a lot better
If we let Jesus be our pacesetter?

He kept priorities in perspective,
Obeying God in ways effective.
What if we'd learn to be content,
And think about how our money is spent?

Would we realize when we have enough,
And quit acquiring extra stuff?
What if instead of keep filling our shelves
We think about others before ourselves?

Crisis: Calm or Chaos?

Emergency Preparedness

What would you do if you woke up one morn
To disaster so great you wish you weren't born?
Could you survive a hurricane or earthquake?
Or would your faith that experience shake?

We are recipients of much blessing,
So I imagine, and I'm only guessing,
That we would quickly prioritize need.
Focus on necessities, not surplus greed.

Safety for family, water, and food,
Are important for my little brood.
Perhaps transportation to get away
From the emergency threatening that day.

Without being paranoid, what could you do,
To prepare for crisis that might involve you?
It helps if you have a savings account,
But keep some cash handy, any amount.

Store important papers in fireproof box
In watertight container that securely locks.
Water and food can be stored away
To be ready for a stormy day.

If you have enough with extra to spare,
Show your neighbors that God's people care.
This might lead to opportunity to share
The awesome God who helped you prepare.

Our coins acknowledge, "In God we Trust".
For our survival, this is a must.
The world's addiction to self-centered greed,
Is what many trust to satisfy need.

But God the Creator is in control
Of all resources, not just the soul.
If we trust Him to help make decisions,
He'll help us prepare extra provisions.

For all who listen to God and obey
He'll help prepare for what's coming our way.
Out of the bad, the Lord will bring good.
In retrospect it will be understood.

Waterfall

I'm just a drop of water
That fell down from the sky.
I joined some other rain drops
In a river passing by.

Happily we skipped along,
Chatting as we went,
Of how we got together
For this comfortable event.

I shared as we related
As coworker, friend, and wife,
Concerned about my pleasures
In my self-fulfilling life.

Skipping with the current
Down the rapidly moving stream,
While often getting knocked about,
I have a lofty dream.

With a full agenda,
Didn't see problems up ahead,
Or thoughts about a waterfall,
I probably would dread.

Suddenly I am falling,
And I begin to shout.
Friends have problems of their own,
So they can't help me out.

Confused, and disoriented,
I fall and churn around.
Frantically I panic.
Cry for help with pleading sound.

Spectators are watching
As I take that scary leap.
They even like it better
When the fall is extra steep.

Eventually this ends
In a calmer stream below.
Nobody seems to notice,
But I like the gentler flow.

Like that drop of water,
In calm times, I will relax.
It's painful in the crisis
With nerves stretched to the max.

I'm helpless when the problems come,
With nothing I can do.
When I need my friends the most,
They're going through crises too.

We need to help each other;
Work together as a team
Until we reach calm waters
Much farther down the stream.

Spectators at a distance
Are amazed at what they see,
Unconcerned with my discomfort
As they are watching me.

They take many pictures
To proudly show their friends
As they describe the waterfall
When their vacation ends.

Eventually I'll recover.
The Lord is in control.
Downstream beyond the turbulence,
Peace will fill my soul.

Indecisive Squirrel

Sitting at the corner, before the children come,
I saw a little squirrel acting rather dumb.
Apparently he was cautioned by his loving mother,
"When you cross the street,
Look one way, then the other."

So the baby squirrel, acting quite obediently,
Scampered to the center to see what he could see.
In the middle of the road,
he stopped to look each way.
When he saw a car, he retreated from his play.

If across the street he wanted to reside,
Why not continue? He was as near the other side.
How often I am just like that little baby squirrel.
After a courageous start, I'm a cautious girl.

Instead of continuing like Jesus told me to,
I tend to retreat, and neglect to follow through.
God grant me the courage to not run away,
But move from my comfort zone
to walk with You today.

Peace and Joy

What in the world will bring me peace?
And what will make my joy increase?
No thing in the world can satisfy.
These come from the Lord; that is why.

When I'm secure relating to Him,
I'm not enticed by a worldly whim.
I don't depend upon job or wealth,
What others think, or physical health.

When events cause moods to rise and fall,
There is no joy or peace at all.
While focusing on God and His love for me,
His peace and joy flow naturally.

Fall Colors

Summertime is over,
And I guess you're dreading fall,
Because you don't appreciate
That painful word at all.

Autumn time is gorgeous,
With its lovely orange and red,
But fall colors are just an ugly
Black and blue instead.

Passing time will turn those bruises
Psychedelic green.
Seniors tend to hibernate
So this beauty isn't seen.

With time and failing memory,
Some things will fade away,
But vividly you'll remember
Your fall the other day.

Of course the Lord anticipated
How you'd look and feel,
So He equipped your body
With what it needs to heal.

Let's Skip Fall This Year

If I must get up at night
It helps to have a tiny light.
I always want to be quite sure
That my footing is secure.

Often old folks tend to slip.
Then they fall and break a hip.
My preference would be not to fall,
For that would be no fun at all.

Bruised Lip and Ego

You think I have a dirty face,
But it's a bruise soap can't erase.
Raking leaves last Saturday,
Compacting the bag so more would stay,
I slipped and fell on a 4 X 4.
Ever since, my lip's been sore.

A baby aspirin every night
Means bruises make an ugly sight.
I'm glad there's no one I must kiss
While my lip still feels like this.
I'll drink from straw or sippy cup
Until this beauty mark heals up.

Each day a different color's there.
The color determines what I wear.
Perhaps my friends will make fun of me
And laugh when my dirty face they see.
I guess I could stay home and hide,
Rather than leave and swallow my pride.

I could hibernate until this ends,
But then I wouldn't see all my friends,
To wish them a Merry Christmas here,
Since I won't see them again this year.
I know I look quite bad today,
But please don't worry, I'm okay.

Cataract Surgery

Gradually with age, my eyes seemed to fade.
Things no longer were clear, I was afraid.
This common eventuality,
Required surgery to clearly see.

Cataract surgery isn't that bad;
Not as painful as others I've had.
I need to remember all of these drops,
To put in my eyes till recovery stops.

Dark glasses I am required to wear
Would not win a prize at a beauty fair.
They are a necessary part of the deal
To keep out bright lights while the eyes heal.

After the cataract surgery,
Everything was bright and clear to me.
Of course that's what I thought it would do,
But I'll be glad when the eye drops are through.

I'm grateful for a good doctor and staff,
And my chauffeur friend who made me laugh.
It was such fun with the first cataract,
I could hardly wait till the next week to go back.

Lesson Learned

I've heard about the frog in the pot,
Who'd jump out if dropped in when it was hot.

But in warm water slowly heated,
Easily he'd be cooked and defeated.

Things began looking blurry to me.
The cataract developed quite gradually.
I thought that my glasses needed a change,
But the lens in my eyes required exchange.

It wasn't until one eye was healing
That I experienced a good new feeling.
One eye was seeing clearly and bright,
While the other still saw a cloudy sight.

This deterioration in my eyesight
Didn't just happen overnight.
Its progression was quite gradual
In my eyes that are weak and fragile.

Had it become cloudy rapidly,
The noticeable difference I would see.
This is what happens when we get off course,
We're unaware of the need for remorse.

We proceed until a painful event
Shows how far from God's will we went.
Often this contrast we fail to see
Till the Great Physician performs surgery.

Then we can see how much more clear
God's plan is to which we should adhere.
We will regret it took a little pain
God's vision and direction to regain.

Flexercize Class

Seven lovely ladies
In the flexercize class,
Moving what we can,
So everyone will pass.

We don't use the hula hoops
Like a little kid,
But then, if we're honest,
We really never did.

We stretch all of our muscles,
As much as we can.
An athletic wannabe,
But just a yoga fan.

The first consideration,
without a single doubt,
Is to "Keep on breathing,
Slowly in and out."

How else could we do it?
We don't really know,
But the teacher tells us
That's the way to go.

Miniature barbells
Strengthen lots of things,
Especially the triceps
Underneath our wings.

When we try to balance,
Some hold on lest they fall.
Definitely the yawn
Is the favorite move of all.

We've flexercized so long,
We know the whole routine.
By now we should be cover girls
On a fitness magazine.

In case you'd like to join us
And have all of this fun,
Come Thursday at eleven.
In an hour we'll be done.

Announcement for Flexercize Class

Some of you would be surprised
How good you'd feel if you exercised.
No promise you'll lose a lot of weight
Or that you won't look like what you ate.
We'll stretch the muscles you forgot you had.
More moveable joints will make you glad.
We move to music as we work each joint.
Staying active is the point.
I'll confess we are to blame
For cheating Arthritis at his game.

Is Pain Free What I Will Always Be?

Jehovah Rapha is the God who heals.
This is a promise that certainly appeals.
How, why, and when cause much debate.
Miraculous healings are always great!

Originally God made a perfect man.
So perfect health is His perfect plan.
But His plan was marred by man's poor choice,
While listening to the tempter's voice.

After God judged that original sin,
New problems began that had not been.
Sickness and death became part of life,
Selfishness, anger, greed, and strife.

God chose a people and gave a command
To put Him first in the promised land.
But sadly His people chose their own way,
So now there is sin in our DNA.

Because God's nature is still the same,
And we can pray in Jesus' Name,
He tells us to ask, to seek, and to knock.
He's always available around the clock.

Many people God will heal;
But when He doesn't, He's just as real.
Sometimes we learn things while we're sick
We wouldn't learn if we got well quick.

We view our pain as a negative thing,
But it is useful to attention bring
To an ailment that is out of sight
So doctors can help to make it right.

Seeking God through His Word and prayer,
You'll discover He really does care.
Listen as His Spirit reveals to you
Something that you can help Him do.

Would a better diet or a little more rest,
Or exercise make your health the best?
Perhaps on your back while you cannot work,
God will surprise you with a welcomed perk.

Whatever God gives you, receive His gift,
Whether physical healing or spiritual lift.
Don't try to tell God what He should do.
Submitting to Him is best for you.

God has a plan for each person He made,
And all our sins were by Jesus paid.
His grace is always sufficient for us.
Don't become a victim or make a fuss.

More serious problems tend to arise
When you think that you're so wise,
And know God's ultimate plan for you,
And try to tell Him what to do.

Suffering

Suffering is normal; it touches each one.
It isn't our choice, and it never is fun.
But sooner or later we all have to face
Circumstances we would rather erase.

It could be tragically losing our health,
Or financial collapse, destroying our wealth.
It may be losing a job or a friend.
Listing all possibilities never would end.

When sharing concerns with friends or with God,
Be real with your feelings, and don't be a fraud.
If you're mad at God, tell Him how you feel.
God can take outbursts if you will be real.

James 1:2-4 says to count it pure joy.
A strong faith in God no trial will destroy.
Perseverance develops as we go through the test,
Maturing our faith as in Jesus we rest.

Romans 5:1-5 says though sufferings increase,
By faith in God's grace we still can have peace.
Rejoice in your suffering and persevere
To develop character with Jesus near.

When light exposes darkness, suffering comes along.
Depending on the Lord will help us be strong.
Ephesians 6:10-18 lists armor we need:
Belt of truth, shield of faith, so we will succeed.

Righteousness the breastplate,
God's Word is the sword,
Helmet of salvation, sharing peace of the Lord.
Since the enemy we can't see or hear,
Stay alert praying, assured God is near.

We'll suffer consequence for a poor choice,
Feel guilty, condemned by the enemy's voice.
God will reveal the escape He had planned.
Confess and repent. God will understand.

Romans 6 reminds us that when we believed,
The old self died when the Lord we received.
Since Jesus arose and still is alive,
We now live with Him—we don't just survive.

Don't follow desires that cause you to sin.
Submit to the Lord and His Spirit within.
You're not under law, sin isn't your master.
Live in God's grace, and you'll mature faster.

Rejoice in the circumstance you are in,
Then the Lord, not the suffering, will win.
Being joyful is difficult to do.
Remember, it's Jesus that we belong to.

Becoming like Jesus is God's plan for us.
He endured pain without resistance or fuss.
If persecuted one day for our Lord,
Suffering with joy will have its reward.

Healthy Balance

Mother at 90 still walked every day,
And she had no medicine bill to pay.
She ate healthy meals and got plenty of rest.
To keep her mind sharp, she liked Scrabble the best.

When I was young, I walked a mile to school,
And exercised summers in a swimming pool.
I learned how to cook and how to bake.
Wholesome meals I could easily make.

Most people could be healthy if they would
Eat nourishing food in the amount they should.
Just think of the difference it would make
If some of these precautions we would take.

Junk food at the store looks good, that is true,
But it really isn't that good for you.
Avoid empty calorie foods that dilute.
Spend your money on veggies and fruit.

Lean meat without additives is a good buy,
But don't select food that you need to deep fry.
Staying out of the chips and soda aisle,
May help avoid the drug counter awhile.

Don't limit exercise to walking in the store,
Unless you want to add a few pounds more.
Gulping fast food for a stomach that's tense
Really does not make very good sense.

One of the ways to enhance your health,
And at the same time conserve your wealth,
Is to sit at your table and take time to eat.
Relaxing with friends for a meal is a treat.

A national problem which I think is sad,
There's always another new dieting fad.
Why aren't people just content to eat less?
To avoid unnecessary overweight stress.

I wonder what Jesus would say today
About problems related to what people weigh.
He offers to carry our impossible load.
Submitting to Him is the secret code.

Calorie Intake −Calories Burned=Calories Stored

Accidents

Pain is More than just Physical.

We hear about accidents every day.
We say "too bad," then go on our way.
But when that accident happens to you,
You find out what the victim goes through.

There are other costs besides the pain;
Mind games playing in your brain,
Medical expenses and loss of wages,
Restricted activities in which one engages.

In times like this you form very close friends,
Who adjust their lives till your crisis ends.
For believers it isn't a total loss,
More time with Jesus, with Him as the Boss.

Going Green

I have fifteen phone books, how about you?
Don't you think just one or two would do?
Books get smaller as folks try to go green,
With numbers so small they can not be seen.
I need a magnifying glass to see.
Could fewer phone books save another tree?

When I was a kid, we had a solar drier.
Between two trees stretched a long piece of wire.
Clothes hung on the wire fastened by a pin.
As soon as they were dry we would bring them in.
People talk about the need for going green,
Have they considered the changes that would mean?

Husband to the Widow

My Lover is always right by my side,
A wonderful Counselor in whom I confide.
He sees the future and gives me direction.
He wants my best, but has grace for imperfection.

I've not gone hungry. God provides all my needs.
When I can't pray, my Lord intercedes.
He's my Protector when I am afraid.
When trouble comes, He is there to give aide.

When I am weak, I just need to ask.
His strength is sufficient for every task.
I fail when I try to do things on my own.
The battle belongs to my Savior alone.

I often don't see how a plan is succeeding,
But later realize that Jesus was leading.
Husband to widows God promised to be.
I'm glad He always has been there for me.

When I had failed, everything had gone wrong,
And my heart broke, He gave me a song.
Like a hurt child when she went out to play,
Close to my Father, that pain went away.

As tears washed away all of my sorrow,
God renewed hope for a brighter tomorrow.
He told me He loved me unconditionally,
And gladly rejoiced as He sang to me.

As I humble myself, and my strivings cease,
He replaces my heartache with His joy and peace.
After these tests I am not quite the same.
Instead of self-focus, I praise His dear Name.

Cooking for One Can Be Fun

I know it is hard to cook for just one,
But really my friend, it can be done.
With the variety, what's best to eat?
Perhaps things in my cart I should delete.

Probably if I would try for a while
To stay out of the snacks and candy aisle,
I would feel better, and weight would decrease,
While cash in my purse would likely increase.

I should consider the way that I shop.
Buying my groceries when hungry must stop.
On empty stomach, all food looks good,
So I buy more groceries than I should.

It helps to take a grocery list.
When in a hurry, essentials aren't missed.
We get confused with all the voices
Giving us so many choices.

While young, I learned a balanced diet
Kept us healthy. Why not still try it?
Fresh fruits and veggies, milk, eggs and meat,
Whole grains, some fat, perhaps something sweet.

We came to meals hungry, for we didn't snack.
We cleaned our plates, and didn't send food back.
We also had time for interaction.
Sharing our day brought satisfaction.

The way food is grown will usually be
The healthiest choice for you and me.
Usually the chemicals added to it
Do not increase nutrition a bit.

I used to try to read every label.
With the small print, I'm no longer able.
The longer the list of additives,
Usually the less food value it gives.

An angel told the apostle Peter,
Who was a strictly kosher eater,
Not to call anything God made unclean,
So I take that admonition to mean,

That usually food in its unaltered form,
Should probably be our daily norm.
So I avoid empty calorie junk food
Unless by so doing, I would be rude.

Since I'm concerned about the price,
Eating sale items each week is nice.
I still prepare for a family of four,
Which provides leftovers for three meals more.

Since I only fix meals that I like to eat,
They still are delicious when I reheat.
This way I have time to get more things done,
And don't have to grab fast food on the run.

Missy

I wanted to help out a friend,
Taking care of her dog this weekend.
So just for fun.
We had a trial run.
On the results, a contract would depend.

Missy seemed to like my back yard.
I thought watching her wouldn't be hard.
She scratched the screen door,
Peed inside on the floor,
And jumped on me and caught me off guard.

Being gone for the hour we planned,
Missy didn't seem to quite understand.
When we got in the car,
We hadn't gone very far,
Till she broke the fence, to look for her land.

We boarded up the hole in the fence.
Then a second departure made sense.
But she opened the gate
And wanted us to wait,
So we padlocked the gate for defense.

We weren't gone for lunch very long.
Thought Missy secure. We were wrong.
Opened gate when we returned,
Showed we hadn't learned,
"Don't Fence Me In" is her favorite song.

Guests

When company comes, to be at my best,
This includes preparation and rest.
If I'm worn out preparing the food,
I may be tired and in a bad mood.

What if everything isn't just so?
Do I think my guests will care, or know?
By planning ahead to simplify,
My guests will have fun, and so will I.

Financial Fitness

When I look at my checkbook and need to trim,
I remember it all belongs to Him.
That gives money a different perspective.
Using it God's way is most effective.

He gave me the talents to get the job.
Forgetting His involvement, would be to rob
My Lord of His primary place in my life.
Selfishly spending brings much stress and strife.

It's not just tithing the ten percent,
But watching where the other ninety went.
Was it to enhance my financial worth?
Or further God's kingdom here on earth?

The money does not belong to me,
So I shouldn't spend it selfishly.
I'll try to save, invest, give, and spend
Wisely for Jesus, who is my Best Friend.

Drastic with Plastic

Do you wonder where the money went,
And how the account got overspent?
Buying on impulse, we often forget
The bill will come due, and we'll be in debt.
Plastic is handy but we need self control,
If financial freedom is our goal.

After vacation my car needs repair.
I have a CD so I don't really care.
I'll shred my plastic and build my account.
I will pay cash so no more debt will mount.
God's my provider: I must work with Him,
Stick to my budget, not buy on a whim.

Being responsible is my intent.
I fear with my plastic I have overspent.
Savings and Social Security should be
Adequate income for a widow like me.
I've become careless along the way
And need to save more for a rainy day.

Attitude Toward Aging

The sunrise reminds me that I'm not the boss,
When early morning I help children cross.
They'd probably make it to school without me,
But probably not quite as confidently.

Some things we control, and some things we can't.
Sometimes we harvest, and sometimes we plant.
We all know old age eventually will come,
So not planning ahead would certainly be dumb.

Our bodies grow weaker; some things we can't do.
We can't control everything, that is true.
But we can control our attitude.
Will we complain or show gratitude?

Will we waste time depressed and comparing?
Or do what we can, gratefully sharing?
Will an offense or need get us off track?
Or be a challenge to quickly attack?

Whatever the issue you're going through,
The choice is ultimately up to you.
The problem won't suddenly go away,
But God's grace is sufficient when you pray.

Caregivers

When there are things your family can't do,
Could you use helpers assisting you?
Making life easier is their goal,
For people unable to be in control.

They specialize in relationships,
And taking clients on medical trips.
Meals or laundry, as previously agreed,
Bathing or dressing, or whatever the need.

You aren't just a client, you are a friend
To caregivers, on whom you can depend.
Whatever will make life better for you,
Is what caregivers are willing to do.

Spring Training

Our Texas Rangers have this thing
Of going to training every spring.
Long before the games begin,
They decide they want to win.

They have work-outs every day
To get in shape so they can play
Their very best as a team,
Since World Series is their dream.

When there is an injured man,
He still works out the best he can.
Returning to full practice soon,
No pity party until June.

I'm just a spectator in the stands,
Concerned about logistic demands—
Like getting a ticket for a good seat,
Comfortable weather, and food to eat.

I yell loud when my team does well,
But visit through a boring spell.
I have the t-shirt. I'm a Rangers fan.
But I don't play like a Rangers man.

Life on earth is like spring training,
Practicing whether sunny or raining.
Some pitch, some catch, but all must run.
Though it's hard work, it can be done.

During the daily practice grind,
I must focus with all my mind
Upon the game I'm preparing for,
To get in shape with plans to score.

Will I be benched or start in the game?
Will I be an asset to Jesus' name?
Will I give up with an injury?
Will I be the best that I can be?

This present life is the practice field,
To see if I will totally yield
To the will of the Eternal Coach,
Or skip practice and bring reproach.

I wonder how it's going to be
When I finally get to see
The Jesus who created me,
And live with Him eternally.

But first the Bible says I must
Learn to put all of my trust
In the Lord who has a plan
For every woman, every man.

My attitude toward God will appear
By how I honor authority here.
If I just obey because I must,
It will be difficult building trust.

I didn't choose my family,
But I can choose my destiny.
If I'm lazy or selfish here,
Will suddenly unselfishness appear?

It is important to follow God's rules,
So in Heaven I'll have the right tools.
With God's love in me, I'll love my brother.
Do I really love God without the other?

If you don't know God, you won't understand
Why I don't do some things you have planned.
But how will you know there's a much better way,
If my life's inconsistent with what I say?

Though not with the Rangers in Surprise,
I am in training. So if I am wise,
I'll get in shape for the final season.
Being with Jesus is the best reason.

When There's a Will, There's a Way To Get Through a Tough Day

You won't get out of this world alive,
So plan ahead to help those who survive.
Not preparing while healthy today
Will complicate matters when you pass away.
These are decisions you'd rather not make,
But are important for your children's sake.
It will help them if you plan ahead,
And not leave everything for the family instead.

Chose an executor for your estate.
This may help them avoid the probate.
When your loved ones are engulfed in grief,
Knowing your wishes will be a relief.
While thinking clearly it is wise
To write a will to avoid a surprise.
A "Do Not Resuscitate" should be planned,
So your wishes the doctor will understand.

Another thing that's usually rough,
Is deciding how to divide your stuff.
Since all will die, it helps to prepare,
So each of your heirs will get his fair share.
Nobody enjoys discussions like this.
Final arrangements they'd rather dismiss.
Till Jesus returns, all people will die.
Reduce family stress when they tell you goodbye.

Time for the Big Move

Around-the-clock care may be required,
Although it's not what you desired.
Everyone struggles with the condition
That requires this major transition.

It is hard to leave the life you have known,
But harder to be unsafe all alone.
Other arrangements need to be made,
Out of your comfort zone, when you're afraid.

We have all seen a mother or father
Put in a home because kids couldn't bother.
We are repulsed by that selfish extreme,
For kids honoring parents is our dream.

But if you need help during the day,
When no one is around, that isn't okay.
Locate a home where there always will be
A skilled caregiver in emergency.

While you're still able, visit a few.
What arrangements will satisfy you?
Is there a pleasant atmosphere?
Did it pass health inspection this year?

Are there activities you like to do?
How does the dinnertime look to you?
Are call bells responded to rapidly?
How is the physical therapy?

Talking to long-time residents
And their families makes good sense.
Linger long enough to see
If a home-like environment there will be.

Assisted Living

With more birthdays than I care to count,
And physical challenges starting to mount,
I'm glad I don't have to live all alone,
Or have to do everything on my own.

I'm glad for the new home where I can be
Safe and secure with my new family.
The part of transition that was very rough,
Was downsizing to get rid of my stuff.

I'm glad there's no longer a big house to clean,
Or lonely days when no friend can be seen.
I like the van so I don't have to drive,
And the good food which helps me to thrive.

If I have a problem, I just have to call;
Immediate help is just down the hall.
In my own room I can be all alone.
I can still talk with old friends on the phone.

Instead of driving to be with my friends
We visit in the lobby, even weekends.
During the week there is chair exercise,
Bingo and crafts and sometimes a surprise.

Therapy helps with muscle restoring.
Varied activities. Life isn't boring.
Young folks are handling all of the chores:
Cleaning and cooking and also outdoors.

Just a new chapter on the journey of life.
I'm now a widow, no longer a wife.
I still have much more living to do.
I'm glad I am getting to do it with you.

Someday when I have finished my race,
I'll move on to my permanent place.
I love the relationship with Jesus here,
So when I go home, I'll have nothing to fear.

God gives opportunity to choose which way
I want to live on this earth each day.
When I do it my way—I'm on my own.
With God in control, I don't walk alone.

Happy Birthday, Sis

What can you expect as you turn 81?
Your golden years should be more fun.
Arthritis prevents threading a needle to sew.
You no longer drive where you want to go.
With memory failing, more meds to remember,
No pressure to teach school again in September.

As a young mother with diapers to change
You never dreamed this day would seem strange.
New challenges in every season of life,
And we get to choose: contentment or strife?
As you celebrate your birthday today,
You observe needs and have time to pray.

God guides and protects though your mate is gone.
You're a child of the King, not a mere pawn.
Enjoy your new friends to the fullest extent
In this new phase of retirement.
Humbly accept help directed your way,
And celebrate YOU on your special day.

Love ya,
Sis

Those Senior Moments

With aging brain cells, I tend to forget
The name of the person whom I just met.
When wanting to use a familiar word,
Out comes a sound that is rather absurd.

A caution for the next generation:
Don't view us seniors with indignation.
Your time is coming and you will regret
How you reacted when we would forget.

You also might want to think ahead
So you won't regret the words that you said.
Like, "I will never do thus and so,"
Or "Why do you old folks move so slow?"

You will remember unfortunately
When you said, "That will never happen to me."
You'll remember hurts you didn't forgive.
Carrying baggage is no way to live.

While your young mind is receptive and clear,
Trust in the Lord, and don't live in fear.
Where there are wrongs, quickly make them right.
Then your senior years will be a delight.

God's Kingdom is Here

We think about God and His Kingdom
As we celebrate Christmas each year.
Other times we focus on problems,
And forget that God's Kingdom is here.

Isaiah foretold His credentials.
To troubled hearts He would bring peace.
Father and Wonderful Counselor,
In a Kingdom that never will cease.

Mary was shocked when the angel
Appeared to bring her the good news.
Joseph believed his dream, though confusing,
The message he dared not refuse.

Angels announced to the shepherds
That they should rejoice and not fear.
God invites everyone to know Him,
It's by faith we each will draw near.

Simeon awaited Messiah,
And recognized Him instantly.
He praised God for this baby of promise
That he had the privilege to see.

When John the Baptist introduced Him,
God's Spirit descended like a dove.
God said, "Listen to my Son Jesus.
He's the pride and joy of my love."

Jesus walked this earth as a human.
He followed God obediently.
His disciples learned ways of the Kingdom
That were available immediately.

The Kingdom of God is now here.
The Kingdom of God is within.
Your relationship with Jesus
Is how all these blessings begin.

He's the Way, the Truth, and the Life.
To God, He's the only way.
He is the Door to the Kingdom,
In spite of what skeptics may say.

Jesus is the Good Shepherd
Who takes good care of His sheep.
He's constantly available,
Watching us while we're asleep.

The Bread of Life that nourishes,
The power that keeps us strong.
The Savior who's willing to rescue,
Although we all have done wrong.

After three years revealing God's Light,
Rejected by self-centered men,
He was crucified and buried.
On the third day He rose again.

His final instruction to disciples
Was to share the Good News as they go.
Jesus would send His Holy Spirit
With power to save and to grow.

How does God's Kingdom affect me?
A relationship close to the Lord.
Humbly submitting to His leading—
He wants me completely on board.

To sum up all the advantages,
Love and acceptance are certainly nice.
Positive hope for daily living.
Security is well worth the price.

So why am I glad I'm a Christian?
As God's child, I'm loved and secure.
I have hope and peace in my soul now,
In a relationship that will endure.

The New Heaven and Earth

God created a perfect heaven and earth,
The people He made didn't choose their birth.
They thought they knew what was best for them,
They disobeyed God, and caused mayhem.

When God creates a new heaven and earth,
He'll let us choose by providing new birth.
Here we decide if we'll live God's way.
He promised to be with us every day.

God always helps when we seek His face.
He lavishes on us His amazing grace.
How we live here affects what we'll do there.
Loving God and others is how we prepare.

If I am negligent and disobey,
I'll have regrets on the judgment day.
I chose adoption in God's family,
I want to serve God here passionately.

I've missed opportunities in the past,
My goal is to serve God up to the last.
Someday I'll meet Jesus, who died so I can live,
And rose to prove He has the power to forgive.

Humor Goes a Long Way

"Old age ain't for sissies," you've probably heard.
Never has there been a truer word.

You can survive with an attitude
That's humble and full of gratitude.

With heart full of love and faith in the Lord,
You'll remain hopeful, not discouraged nor bored.

As your body slows down and returns to dust,.
Learning to laugh at yourself is a must.

About the Author and Book

When you read my book, I want you to know
That I'm not quite this feeble from head to toe.
This book is non-fiction, so content is true.
There's poetic license in a place or two.
I write each poem with someone in mind,
Then make it generic so it will be kind.
I'm a young lady—still in my prime.
I'm just 39—for the 39th time.
As years roll by I'm more cautious than bold.
But whatever your age, *You're* still *Not Too Old*.

Made in the USA
Lexington, KY
13 March 2018